WITHDRAWN

TRAVEL WITH THE GREAT EXPLORERS

Explore with

Ferdinand Magellan

Marie Powell

Crabtree Publishing Company
www.crabtreebooks.com

Crabtree Publishing Company
www.crabtreebooks.com

Author: Marie Powell
Publishing plan research
     and development: Reagan Miller
Managing Editor: Tim Cooke
Editors: Crystal Sikkens, Shannon Welbourn
Designer: Lynne Lennon
Picture Manager: Sophie Mortimer
Design Manager: Keith Davis
Editorial Director: Lindsey Lowe
Children's Publisher: Anne O'Daly
Production coordinator
     and prepress technician: Tammy McGarr
Print coordinator: Katherine Berti

Produced by Brown Bear Books for
Crabtree Publishing Company

Photographs:
Front Cover: Shutterstock: tr, br, Steve Estvanik cr;
Thinkstock: Photos.com main.

Interior: Alamy: Lebrecht Music and Arts Photo Library 11,
Mary Evans Picture Library 10, North Wind Picture Archives 12,
16b, 18, Prisma Archivo 29l, The Art Archive 28t; Clipart: 13b;
Lesley FW: 15b; Mary Evans Picture Library: 5t, 19t, 24-25b;
Public Domain: 14-14b, 25b, Abdulla Hamidin 20; Robert Hunt
Library: 4, 5b, 13t, 27bl; Shutterstock: 7br, 21b, 26, Andrey Burmakin
25t, Filpe Frazao 21t, Eric Isselée 21r, Anton Ivanov 7tl, Marina Jay
26t, Anan Kaewkhammul 28b, Somyot Pattana 17br, Vibrant Image
Studio 19b, Valentyn Volkov 23br; Mirko Thiessen: 23t;
Thinkstock: Hemera 29r, istockphoto 6, 17b, 22tl, 22br,
Stocktrek Images 25t.

All other artwork and maps © Brown Bear Books Ltd.

Brown Bear Books has made every attempt to contact the
copyright holder. If you have any information please contact
licensing@brownbearbooks.co.uk

Library and Archives Canada Cataloguing in Publication

Powell, Marie, author
     Explore with Ferdinand Magellan / Marie Powell.

(Travel with the great explorers)
Includes index.
Issued in print and electronic formats.
ISBN 978-0-7787-1425-5 (bound).--ISBN 978-0-7787-1431-6 (pbk.).--
ISBN 978-1-4271-7582-3 (pdf).--ISBN 978-1-4271-7576-2 (html)

     1. Magalhfaes, Fernfao de, -1521--Juvenile literature.
2. Explorers--Portugal--Biography--Juvenile literature.
3. Voyages around the world--Juvenile literature. I. Title.

G420.M2P78 2014   j910'.92   C2014-903748-1
                                           C2014-903749-X

Library of Congress Cataloging-in-Publication Data

Powell, Marie, 1958-
 Explore with Ferdinand Magellan / Marie Powell.
     pages cm. -- (Travel with the great explorers)
 Includes index.
 ISBN 978-0-7787-1425-5 (reinforced library binding) --
 ISBN 978-0-7787-1431-6 (pbk.) --
 ISBN 978-1-4271-7582-3 (electronic pdf) --
 ISBN 978-1-4271-7576-2 (electronic html)
 1. Magalhães, Fernão de, -1521--Juvenile literature. 2. Explorers-
-Portugal--Biography--Juvenile literature. 3. Voyages around the
world--Juvenile literature. I. Title.

G286.M2P68 2015
910.4'1--dc23
                                           2014020965

Crabtree Publishing Company

www.crabtreebooks.com   1-800-387-7650

Printed in Hong Kong/082014/BK20140613

Copyright © **2015 CRABTREE PUBLISHING COMPANY**. All rights reserved. No part of this publication may be reproduced, stored
in a retrieval system or be transmitted in any form or by any means, electronic, mechanical, photocopying, recording, or otherwise,
without the prior written permission of Crabtree Publishing Company. In Canada: We acknowledge the financial support of the
Government of Canada through the Canada Book Fund for our publishing activities.

Published in Canada
Crabtree Publishing
616 Welland Ave.
St. Catharines, ON
L2M 5V6

Published in the United States
Crabtree Publishing
PMB 59051
350 Fifth Avenue, 59th Floor
New York, New York 10118

Published in the United Kingdom
Crabtree Publishing
Maritime House
Basin Road North, Hove
BN41 1WR

Published in Australia
Crabtree Publishing
3 Charles Street
Coburg North
VIC, 3058

CONTENTS

Prima ego velivolis ambivi curzibus Orbem,
Magellane novo te duce ducta freto.
Ambivi, meritoq vocor VICTORIA: sunt mi
Vela, alæ; precium, gloria; pugna, mare.

Meet the Boss

Did you know?

In 1505, Ferdinand and Diogo Magellan signed up for a large Portuguese expedition to East Africa and India as unpaid "gentlemen adventurers."

Ferdinand Magellan was a Portuguese explorer. Believing Earth was round, he led the first voyage around the world.

PORTUGUESE CHILDHOOD

+ Explorer serves as a royal page

Ferdinand Magellan belonged to a noble but poor family in Portugal. After his parents died, when he was only 10 years old, he moved to Lisbon with his brother Diogo. Ferdinand became a **page** in the royal court, and got an education. He witnessed Portugal's great age of exploration—and decided to become an explorer.

PIG-HEADED

☛ **Captain is stubborn**

☛ **Upsets his colleagues**

Magellan was a very determined man. He stuck to his course even when others told him to give up, so some called him stubborn. But he was also a devout Christian and was very loyal to his men.

> Our mirror, our light, our comforter, our true guide."
> *Sailor Antonio Pigafetta describes Magellan.*

FIGHTING FOR THE FAITH

★ **Young knight fights Muslims**

★ **Falls out with king**

Magellan went into military service for Portugal. He fought **Muslim** forces in East Africa and helped Portugal conquer Melaka in Malaysia and make it a **colony**. But Magellan did not get along with King Manuel of Portugal. King Manuel refused several times to give Magellan command of a ship to sail to the Spice Islands. So, feeling frustrated, Magellan asked to be dismissed from service so he could look for another country to support his quest to sail to the Spice Islands.

ASIA!

By a treaty of 1494 between Spain and Portugal, Portugal claimed the Spice Islands (now the Moluccas). Magellan believed they might belong to Spain, instead.

SWITCHING SIDES

☛ **Explorer sails on behalf of Spain**

☛ **Portuguese king furious**

After he left Portuguese service, Magellan moved to Spain with his friend, Duarte Barbosa. Magellan married Duarte's sister, Beatriz Caldeira Barbosa, and they had two children. Magellan's father-in-law introduced him to King Charles I of Spain (right). Charles agreed to fund Magellan's exploration and allowed him to look for a route to the famed Spice Islands.

My Explorer Journal

★ **King Manuel of Portugal was furious when Magellan sailed in the service of the Spanish king. Use details in the text to write a letter on Magellan's behalf, defending his decision.**

Where Are We Heading?

GO ROUND!

Magellan's was the first expedition to sail around the world, but by the time of his voyage all educated Europeans knew the world was round.

Magellan's voyage took him down the coast of South America and through a narrow strait—now called the Strait of Magellan—into the Pacific Ocean. He sailed across the vast ocean to the Philippines.

ACROSS THE ATLANTIC

- Exploring South America
- Looking for a route west

On August 10, 1519, Magellan set sail leading five ships to cross the Atlantic. They went to Rio de Janeiro in Brazil, then sailed south to Argentina, where they spent the winter of 1520. After months at sea, Magellan's tired and hungry crew tried to **mutiny**. Magellan was able to defeat them and carry on with his voyage.

Did you know?

Many European explorers set off to find a western sea route to Asia. Most searched for a Northwest Passage around the top of North America.

LIFE OF FIRES

★ **Explorer finds sea channel**

★ **Sees mysterious lights**

From late October through November in 1520, Magellan sailed through a passage between the Atlantic and Pacific oceans. Today it is known as the **Strait** of Magellan. One story says Magellan saw native campfires on the shore. He named the region Tierra de los Fuegos, or land of fires. Today it is known as Tierra del Fuego (left).

EYES ON THE PRIZE

+ Spice Island destination

+ Big rewards for new route

In the 1500s, Europeans prized Asian **spices** not just for their taste, but also because they thought spices would help keep their food from spoiling and even prevent disease. The overland trade routes to Asia were controlled by Muslims and traders from Venice, Italy. They kept the price of spices in Europe high. European traders wanted to gain control of the spice trade. They thought it would be possible to sail west to find a sea route to the Spice Islands. That was Magellan's aim when he began his voyage.

🌧 Weather Forecast

KEEP CALM

At the end of November in 1520, Magellan sailed into the unknown Pacific Ocean he named Mar Pacifico or "calm sea." The ocean, however, could be very violent. Travelers had to look out for typhoons, or tropical storms. Tsunamis **were another threat.**

Magellan's Voyage Around the World

The journey around the world took Magellan to many places no Europeans had visited. Only a skilled navigator could have made such a voyage successfully—and Magellan came close to failing a number of times.

NORTH AMERICA

ATLANTIC OCEAN

SOUTH AMERICA

PACIFIC OCEAN

ATLANTIC OCEAN

Rio de Janeiro

As they sailed down the coast of South America, Magellan's crew searched for a route to the Pacific Ocean. They anchored in the bay at Rio de Janeiro, which had been discovered by the Portuguese in 1502.

Puerto San Julián

Magellan spent the winter of 1520 in southern Argentina. It was bitterly cold. One of his ships, the *Santiago*, sank in a storm and he had to defeat a mutiny against him led by some of the captains of his ships.

Strait of Magellan

Magellan took over a month to sail through the passage in Tierra del Fuego that is now named for him. While he explored the narrow channel, one of his ships, the *San Antonio*, turned around and headed back to Spain—taking most of his supplies.

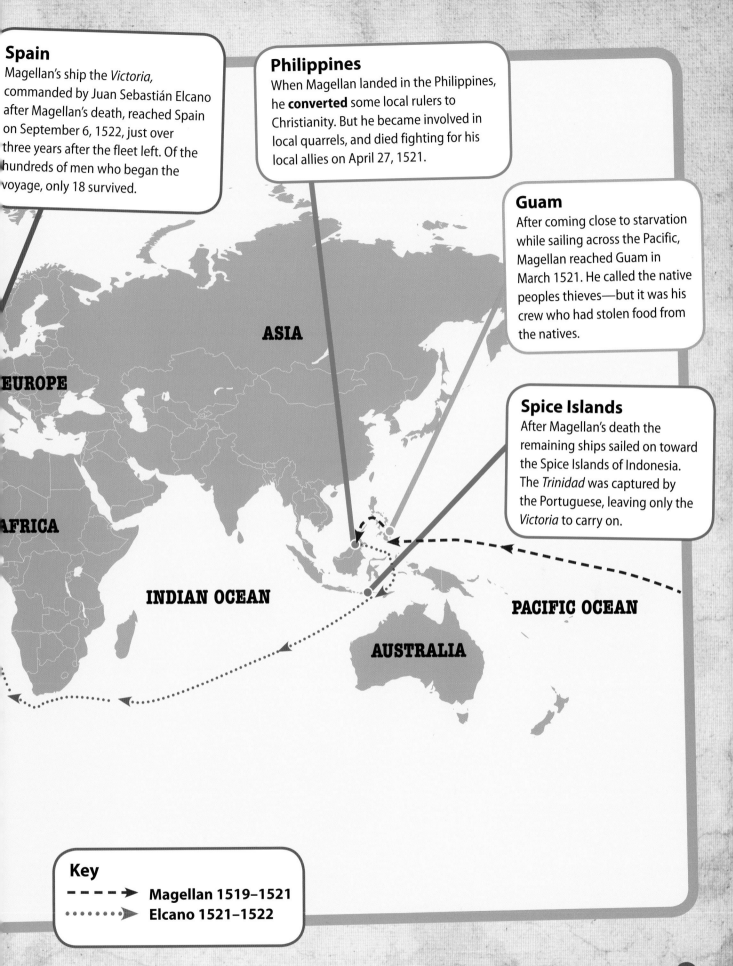

Spain
Magellan's ship the *Victoria*, commanded by Juan Sebastián Elcano after Magellan's death, reached Spain on September 6, 1522, just over three years after the fleet left. Of the hundreds of men who began the voyage, only 18 survived.

Philippines
When Magellan landed in the Philippines, he **converted** some local rulers to Christianity. But he became involved in local quarrels, and died fighting for his local allies on April 27, 1521.

Guam
After coming close to starvation while sailing across the Pacific, Magellan reached Guam in March 1521. He called the native peoples thieves—but it was his crew who had stolen food from the natives.

Spice Islands
After Magellan's death the remaining ships sailed on toward the Spice Islands of Indonesia. The *Trinidad* was captured by the Portuguese, leaving only the *Victoria* to carry on.

ASIA

EUROPE

AFRICA

INDIAN OCEAN

PACIFIC OCEAN

AUSTRALIA

Key
- – – ➤ **Magellan 1519–1521**
- •••••➤ **Elcano 1521–1522**

Meet the Crew

As a Portuguese sailor in the service of the Spanish crown, Magellan had many enemies—including his own Spanish captains, who led a mutiny against him.

TOO SICK

★ **Magellan's partner stays at home**

The Portuguese geographer and **astronomer** Rui de Faleiro (Ruy Faleiro) was the first person to talk about the existence of a strait through South America that led to the Pacific. He helped Magellan plan the voyage. However, he was too sick to go on the expedition itself.

MUTINY!

+ **Captains plot against Magellan**

+ **Ringleaders executed**

Magellan's Spanish captains did not like their leader. Juan de Cartagena, captain of the *San Antonio*, led a mutiny to take control of the fleet. Magellan used loyal men to kill one of the rebel captains. He sentenced the other mutineers to death, torture, or hard labor. Cartagena and another man were **marooned** on an island in the Pacific. They were never heard from again, and Magellan restored his authority.

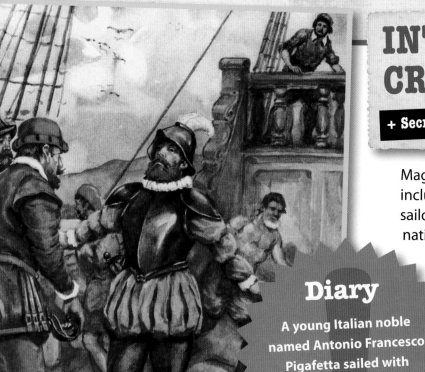

INTERNATIONAL CREW

+ Secret destination

Magellan's crew of over 250 men included Portuguese and Spanish sailors, as well as men of various nationalities, among them Greek, German, Dutch, African, French, and Italian. These sailors did not know their destination until the voyage had begun.

Diary

A young Italian noble named Antonio Francesco Pigafetta sailed with Magellan on the *Trinidad*. His diary of the expedition became famous.

ROYAL FRIEND

☞ Can Spain claim the Spice Islands?

The young Spanish king, King Charles I, was eager to get an advantage in the exploration of the Pacific Ocean and a route to Asia. In 1494, a treaty was signed dividing newly discovered land between Spain and Portugal. The world was divided by a line that ran north to south through the Atlantic Ocean. New land to the west of the line belonged to Spain and land to the east belonged to Portugal. Magellan told King Charles that his calculations showed the Spice Islands belonged to Spain. That helped convince the king to **sponsor** his expedition.

ROYAL ENEMY

★ **Young men fall out**

★ **Quarrel changes history**

When Magellan was a boy, Duke Manuel had been in charge of the school for pages. He disliked Magellan then, and continued to dislike him as he got older. When the duke became King of Portugal and heard that Magellan was sailing on behalf of Spain, he sent spies and ships to try to stop Magellan's mission—but he failed.

Check Out the Ride

Magellan was given a fleet of five ships to make the voyage. They were so old it took a year to prepare them—and Portuguese spies tried to disrupt his plans.

Did you know?

The Portuguese sent agents to try to delay Magellan. They paid merchants not to deal with him, so he could not buy the supplies he needed.

FIVE-SHIP FLEET

☛ Repairs delay voyage a year

☛ Provisions run short

Magellan's fleet of five vessels was called the Armada de Molucca. The ships were old, however, and it took over a year to repair them, take on supplies, and hire the crew. Portuguese spies tried to slow down the work. After Magellan set out, he found he had fewer **provisions** than he had ordered.

FLAGSHIP SAILS AHEAD

+ Reluctant to serve a foreign commander

As Magellan's **flagship**, the *Trinidad*, sailed in front of the fleet, leading the way. Magellan ordered the captains of the other ships to follow the *Trinidad*'s signal flags and torches. One reason for the Spanish captains' **plot** against Magellan was that they didn't want to take orders from a Portuguese commander.

WHAT BECAME OF THE SHIPS?

★ **And then there was one**

★ **Ill-fated voyage**

Only one of the five ships made the whole voyage. The *Santiago* sank while exploring in South America. The *San Antonio* abandoned the fleet and turned back to Spain. After Magellan's death, the *Concepción* was burned because there were not enough men left to sail it. Later, the Portuguese captured the captain and crew of the *Trinidad*. Only the *Victoria*, with 18 survivors, made it home to Spain.

Prima ego velivolis ambivi cursibus Orbem,
Magellane novo te duce ducta freto.
Ambivi, meritoqz vocor VICTORIA: sunt mî
Vela, alæ; precium, gloria; pugna, mare.

CARAVEL

☞ **Speedsters of the sea**

☞ **Easy to handle**

Magellan's smallest ship, the *Santiago*, was likely a **caravel**. It had triangular sails that could be angled to allow it to sail into the wind. Caravels were small, fast, and easy to maneuver. They also had enough room to be useful for carrying cargo.

Solve It with Science

Magellan was an outstanding navigator. He made the best use of the tools available. He also learned from other Europeans who had sailed to the Americas.

Sandy

An hourglass consisted of two glass bulbs joined by a narrow neck. Sand dribbled slowly through the neck. It too 30 minutes to flow from one bulb to the other.

NAVIGATING THE ROUTE

★ **Watch where you're going**

★ **Dead reckoning rocks**

Dead reckoning is an estimate of the ship's speed and distance from a known point such as a landmark. This estimate was checked by the positions of the stars and corrected in case of changes in wind or currents. The sailors watched where they were going very carefully. Time was counted using an hourglass or sand clock. It took 30 minutes for the sand to empty into the bottom bulb. This was called a glass. Eight glasses (four hours) was known as a watch.

> There was no man alive who understood more than he abo the sciences of cartography ar navigation."
>
> *Antonio Pigafetta on Magellan.*

LOOKING FOR THE ROUTE

☞ **Maps lack detail**

☞ **Is there a way through?**

Many explorers were searching for *El Paso*, the name given to a possible pass, or route, through South America. Magellan studied the most recent maps and logs he could find to try to discover where it might be. None of them had detailed information. The first map to show the "**New World**," by Juan de la Cosa (right), was only drawn in 1500.

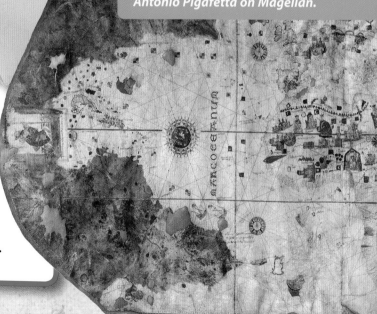

NEW PHENOMENON

- ☞ **Clouds in the heavens**
- ☞ **Glimpses of distant galaxies**

Near the **equator** in the Southern Hemisphere, Magellan and his crew saw what they called two "clouds of mist" in the night sky. These so-called Magellanic Clouds are far off in space. We now know they are formed by the stars of distant galaxies. Magellan was the first European to see them.

IT'S IN THE STARS

- ★ **Pictures in the sky**
- ★ **Cutting edge technology**

Stars and constellations showed sailors the ship's **latitude**, or its position north or south of the equator. Sailors also used a device called an **astrolabe**, which measured the height of the Sun above the horizon, to calculate their position more exactly.

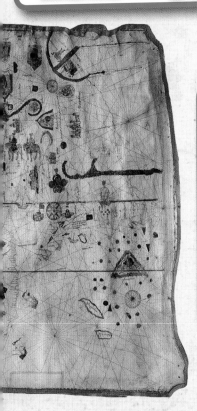

TOOL KIT

+ Modern devices available

Magellan and his captains had the most modern navigational tools available for the time. This included a **cross-staff** for measuring the height of the sun or stars above the horizon, and a compass. The compass always pointed toward north, to help sailors find their way.

Hanging at Home

For Magellan and his men, home was mainly onboard their ships. They were often wet and cold, and short on sleep. They frequently came close to running out of food.

TRAVEL UPDATE

More please!

★ On a long voyage, it was important to take along enough food—and some blankets. Everyone slept on deck except the captain. Sailors had to watch out for worms in the ship's biscuits or for water that turned yellow and foul. When they ran out of food, Magellan's men caught rats to eat and even ate sawdust.

> "Rats were so much in request, that we paid half a ducat apiece for them."
> *Antonio Pigafetta on conditions in the Pacific.*

FIRE! FIRE!

★ **Ghostly lights on ship**

★ **Terrifying sight**

During a storm off the coast of Africa, a fire-like glow appeared on the ships' masts and rigging. This was caused by electricity in the atmosphere, but the terrified sailors believed it was a sign of St. Elmo, protector of sailors. The phenomenon is called St. Elmo's fire.

WINTER CONDITIONS

The ships sailed toward the Antarctic region in wintry conditions. Hail and sleet made decks slippery. The freezing salt water chafed the sailors' skin and made their clothes brittle. It even caused frostbite, which could make fingers or toes fall off.

 My Explorer Journal

★ **Imagine that you are extremely hungry onboard a ship, like one of Magellan's men. What kind of food do you think you would think about most often? Give reasons for your choices.**

WINTER CAMP

+ Mutiny in the snow

+ Hunting for food

In March 1520, Magellan and his crew camped for the winter in Puerto San Julián, in what is now southern Argentina. The men built huts from wood on the shore. Their supplies were low, so Magellan cut the crew's daily **rations**. They had to hunt and fish for food. This angered the Spanish captains and crew and led to their mutiny against Magellan, but Magellan defeated them.

PACIFIC LARDER

☛ Explorers find supplies...

☛ ...but run short of water

Magellan's fleet passed many Pacific islands without seeing them. Even though the ocean was full of fish, they had no nets to catch them. They were starving when they finally found an uninhabited island, where they gathered fresh fish, crabs, and seabirds, as well as fresh water. When these supplies ran out, they came close to starvation again. They found more food on the island of Guam, including coconuts and bananas.

The Pacific Ocean

Europeans knew the Pacific Ocean existed—but Magellan was the first man to explore it. It was far, far bigger than he or anyone else had ever imagined.

THE NEW OCEAN

☛ **First sighting of the Pacific**

☛ **How do we get there?**

By the time of Magellan's voyage, Europeans already knew there was an ocean beyond the Americas. In 1513, the Spanish explorer Vasco Núñez de Balboa climbed a hill in the narrow neck of Panama and saw the Pacific Ocean for the first time. The news convinced Magellan that he would be able to find a route from the Atlantic to the Pacific—and then to Asia.

THE WAY THROUGH

★ **Wintry channel challenges sailors**

★ **Where does it lead?**

The Strait of Magellan is a 334-mile (534 km) passage that runs through mountains and glaciers. It has narrow areas, islands, high tides, and strong currents. It took Magellan's fleet over a month to sail through it to the Pacific. There, Magellan learned that the *San Antonio* had not sailed up ahead as he instructed, but rather sailed back to Spain with most of his supplies.

VALUABLE BREAKTHROUGH

+ Southwest Passage found!

+ New route to Asia

Magellan's discovery of a southwest passage promised great trade benefits to Spain, as long as the route from South America to Asia was as short as he expected. Unfortunately, it was far too long to be a useful trade route.

Too big

Magellan misjudged the size of the world—but so did other explorers. Christopher Columbus also believed the world was much smaller than it actually is.

WHAT'S IN A NAME?

☛ New ocean not always calm

☛ No joy for sailors

Magellan named the new ocean "Pacific," meaning calm or peaceful waters. It turned out to be Earth's largest ocean—and its waters are not always peaceful. Magellan and his men faced accidents, sickness, fighting, and hunger. They went for nearly four months without fresh food and water. Their voyage was anything but calm.

> I do not believe there is in this world a more beautiful and better strait than this one!"
> *Antonio Pigafetta on the Strait of Magellan.*

Meeting and Greeting

Magellan met local peoples in South America and on the islands in the Pacific. When he reached the Philippines, he had the advantage of having a servant who could speak local languages.

LOYAL SERVANT

- Slave helps explorer
- Tricked out of freedom

While he was in military service, Magellan acquired a personal slave named Enrique, who was also referred to as Henry, from Portugal's colony in Melaka. Enrique accompanied Magellan on his voyage. When they reached the Philippines, Enrique could speak the natives' language and acted as a translator. Magellan's **will** stated that Enrique should be freed after Magellan's death. However, when the time came, the captains refused to free him. In return, Enrique plotted with rulers in the Philippines to set a trap for them.

Melaka

Melaka became a Portuguese colony in 1511. It was likely at this time that Enrique became Magellan's slave. Today, Melaka is part of Malaysia in Southeast Asia.

GIANTS IN SOUTH AMERICA

- ★ Are they really that tall?
- ★ Dangerous to explorers

Magellan and his crew described a race of giants in Patagonia, in southern Argentina. They said they saw people of "giant stature," with painted yellow and red faces. Magellan named them Patagonians, but they may have been Tehuelches, a native tribe in Paragonia. He tried to capture some people, but they fought him off.

FRIENDLY CANNIBALS

+ Don't eat me

+ Let's try a parrot instead

In Rio de Janiero, Magellan met native people called the Guarani. Although the Guarani were **cannibals**, they befriended Magellan and his crew, who spent two weeks in the area. The crew traded with the Guarani for food and animals such as parrots and monkeys.

Did you know?

Magellan knew he had reached the Philippines because Enrique called out in the Malay language and the islanders answered.

HANDS OFF!

☞ **Island of thieves**

On Guam, Magellan and his crew mistook the curiosity of the Chamorros people—who had no concept of personal ownership—for greed. He named Guam the Island of Thieves. The Europeans, weakened by scurvy, wanted to go ashore. Instead, the islanders came aboard and stripped the ship. Magellan fired his cannons which scared them away. Then his men went ashore and killed some Chamorros, and stole food from them.

I Love Nature

During the long voyage, Magellan and his men were the first Europeans to see many plants and animals that were unknown outside South America. Some are now known by his name.

STRANGE ANIMALS

★ **Camels without humps**

★ **Wolves in the sea**

Antonio Pigafetta's diary of the voyage describes a number of strange animals. He calls some "camels without humps." They may have been **guanaco**. He said other animals had mule ears and camel necks—they may have been llamas. He also described "sea wolves" with calf heads, large teeth, and human-like hands—likely sea lions.

BIRDS OF A FEATHER

+ Are they really geese?

Among the animals Pigafetta recorded, he described featherless black geese. He said they had to be skinned rather than plucked like normal geese. They were most likely penguins. They were later named Magellanic penguins after Magellan.

NEW BIOME, NEW SPECIES

☛ **Sailors less interested in science...**

☛ **... More interested in food**

The Strait of Magellan is in a subpolar region at the southern end of Chile and Argentina, near Tierra del Fuego. Many animal and bird species live in this forested region, which is now known as the Magellanic subpolar forest. They include the cougar and the Patagonian chinchilla mouse. Magellan's men stocked up on fish, birds, and other wild animals they found before their journey into the uncharted Pacific Ocean.

Did you know?

The Magellanic subpolar forests are the most southerly forests in the world. They include evergreen and deciduous forests.

My Explorer Journal

★ **Using the bottom photograph on page 22, describe a Magellanic penguin as if you were writing to someone who has never seen one before.**

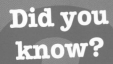

PRIZED SPICES

★ **Plants worth weight in gold**

★ **Europeans love spices**

The only ship that survived Magellan's voyage was the *Victoria*. It carried home a cargo of cloves and other spices. The Europeans prized spices such as peppercorn, nutmeg, cinnamon, and cloves. The spices brought back on the *Victoria* were worth more than twice the cost of Magellan's voyage.

Fortune Hunting

Magellan knew that if he was successful in finding a new sea route to the Spice Islands of Asia, he would become immensely wealthy. So would the Spanish crown.

Silk Road

Most spices reached Europe by an overland trade route called the Silk Road. Muslim kingdom and the Italian state of Venice charged high taxes on all trade along the route.

TRAVEL UPDATE

Opens new way to East

★ If Magellan discovered a trade route to the Spice Islands that would allow Spain to avoid the Muslim and Venetian **monopoly** over trade through Asia, it would be a rich source of income for the Spaniards—and for Magellan.

DEAL WITH THE KING

☛ **Explorer robbed by death**

☛ **Family gets nothing**

Magellan's deal with King Charles would have given the explorer the rights to many of the new lands he discovered. That would have made him a fortune. He would also have shared one-fifth of the expedition's profits, while the king would have received the rest. However, after Magellan's death his family did not receive any of the promised fortune.

DIFFERENT SORT OF WEALTH

+ Souls as important as gold

+ Explorer spreads faith

As a devout Christian, Magellan wanted to make Christian converts in the Philippines— their souls were a different sort of "wealth." Magellan's Easter Sunday Mass impressed Rajah Colambu, king of the island of Limasawa, who erected a cross on a hill. On the island of Cebu, Rajah Humabon and his wife asked to be baptized as Christians, followed by 500 men and 50 women.

> " I hope that the renown of such a high-spirited captain will never be forgotten."
> *Antonio Pigafetta on Magellan.*

GOLD GALORE

★ **Jewelry gives clue**

★ **Rich supplies of precious metal**

Although Magellan was most interested in bringing back valuable spices, he found that the Philippines had a rich source of gold. He landed on an island where the rajah, or king, wore gold ornaments, so Magellan began trading.

This Isn't What It Said in the Brochure!

Many parts of Magellan's journey were difficult. His men put up with hunger, shortage of water, and disease—as well as uncertainty about where they were heading.

Did you know?

Scurvy was a disease suffered by many sailors on long voyages. It could be fatal. It was caused by a lack of Vitamin C, since a sailor's diet included no fresh fruit, only salted fish and meat.

THE PACIFIC

★ **Food runs short**

While traveling along the Pacific Ocean, the ships' food spoiled and the water became undrinkable. Many of the men got scurvy. After four months, they reached an island where they took on fresh supplies.

THE DOLDRUMS

☞ **Going nowhere fast**

☞ **No wind for days**

Near the equator, Magellan's ships became stuck for three weeks without wind in an area now known as the Doldrums. Sailing ships relied on wind to move, so the fleet drifted. Magellan had to cut the sailor's rations of food and water to make them last longer.

LOCAL FIGHT

+ Explorer joins local squabbles

+ Fights to spread Christianity

Magellan converted Rajahs Humabon and Colambu to Christianity. But he became angry when the ruler of Mactan, Lapu-Lapu, refused to convert or to acknowledge Spanish rule. On April 27, 1521, he took about 50 volunteers from his fleet and sailed to Mactan.

Islands

In the Philippines, Magellan had become allies with the rulers of some islands. But Lapu-Lapu would not swear to obey the Spanish king, so Magellan set out to defeat him by force.

Victoria

My Explorer Journal

★ **Imagine that you are stuck on a small ship in the middle of the ocean for three weeks. Think of ways that you and your crew members could pass the time.**

DEATH ON THE BEACH

☛ **Magellan killed**

☛ **Dies protecting men**

Lapu-Lapu's men outnumbered Magellan and his crew. Magellan ordered his men to retreat to the ships. He, Enrique, and Pigafetta fought on while the men escaped. Magellan was surrounded and killed. His body was never recovered.

End of the Road

After Magellan's death there were only enough men left to sail two ships, so the *Concepción* was burned. The other two vessels headed for home—but only one would make it.

LEAVING THE PHILIPPINES

☛ Captains flee for their lives

After Magellan died, Enrique helped the Philippine rajahs capture some of the ships' captains. The others fled. Joao Lopes Carvalho took over. He ordered Magellan's papers be burned to cover up the earlier mutiny.

THE WAY HOME

★ Did crew become pirates?

★ Cargo of spices

Under Carvalho, the crews of the *Trinidad* and *Victoria* may have become pirates along the Philippine coast. Eventually they came to the Spice Islands, where the sultan, or ruler, gave them a valuable cargo of cloves and other spices. Gonzalo Gomez Espinosa, an officer who was loyal to Magellan, became captain of the *Trinidad*. But when the ship stopped for repairs in Portuguese waters, most of the crew were captured by the Portuguese.

STAND-IN CAPTAIN

+ Survivor takes the credit...

Juan Sebastian del Cano (Elcano) finally sailed the *Victoria* home to Spain in 1522 with only 18 survivors and a cargo of cloves and other spices. At first, the former mutineer took credit for the voyage. He gained himself a royal **pension**—but nothing for the sailors who returned with him. Magellan's wife and children had died, but the rest of his family received nothing from the voyage. Pigafetta's diary and other surviving documents eventually helped set the record straight.

My Explorer Journal

★ **Imagine you are one of the survivors of the voyage returning home after more than three years away. How would you have reacted to reaching your homeland?**

Did you know?

The captain of the *Trinidad* kept a log of the voyage. His account supported what Pigafetta described. They showed the credit for the voyage belonged to Magellan.

CHANGING THE WORLD

★ **Explorer's fame spreads**

Magellan's story circulated widely thanks to an account of the voyage published in 1524 by Antonio Pigafetta. Pigafetta said Magellan had natural talent and courage. He hid the mutiny of the Spanish captains at first, but eventually the full story came out. The voyage helped people realize just how large the world really is.

GLOSSARY

astrolabe An instrument that measured the height of the Sun or Moon above the horizon

astronomer Someone who studies the stars and other heavenly bodies

cannibal A person that eats human flesh

caravel A small, fast-sailing ship used in Spain and Portugal from the 1400s to the 1600s

colony A country or area that is governed by another country

convert To persuade someone to change their religion

cross-staff A device used to measure the height of stars or the Sun above the horizon

ducat A European gold coin

equator An imaginary line that runs around the middle of Earth

flagship The ship that carries the admiral who commands a fleet

guanaco A wild mammal from Patagonia that resembles a llama

latitude How far a location on Earth is north or south of the equator

maroon To put someone ashore on a deserted island and abandon them

Muslim Someone who observes the Islamic religion

mutiny A rebellion against authority, particularly by soldiers or sailors against officers

New World The name given to North, Central, and South America by Europeans after they discovered these lands existed

page A young man being trained to become a knight

pension A regular payment made to support someone in old age

plot A secret plan to do something illegal

provisions Storages of food and drink

ration A fixed amount or portion, such as food

spices Plants such as pepper or cinnamon that are used to flavor food

sponsor To pay for and help organize an event

strait A narrow passage of water connecting two larger bodies of water

tsunami A large wave triggered by an earthquake beneath the ocean

will A document that says what should happen to someone's possessions after his or her death

Magellan is born to a noble but poor family in Portugal with connections to the royal court.

Magellan takes part in the Portuguese conquest of Melaka, in Malaysia. He acquires a Malay servant, name Enrique.

August 10: Magellan and his five ships leave Spain and head across the Atlantic Ocean to South America.

September: Magellan defeats a mutiny against him by the Spanish captains of his ships.

1480 **1490** **1492** **1511** **1512** **1519** **1520**

Magellan's parents die.

Magellan enters the service of the royal family as a page.

Magellan begins to plan a voyage. When the Portuguese king refuses to support him, he moves to Spain.

March: The fleet anchor for the winter at Puerto San Julián in southern Argentina.

ON THE WEB

www.bbc.co.uk/history/historic_ figures/magellan_ferdinand.shtml
A biography of Magellan from BBC History.

www.enchantedlearning.com/ explorers/page/m/magellan.shtml
A page on Magellan from Enchanted Learning, together with a fun activity sheet.

www.history.com/topics/exploration/ ferdinand-magellan
History.com biography of Magellan.

www.livescience.com/42788- ferdinand-magellan.html/
Live Science biography of Magellan, with a map of his circumnavigation.

BOOKS

Aretha, David. *Magellan: First to Circle the Globe* (Great Explorers of the World). Enslow Publishers, 2009.

Bailey, Katharine. *Ferdinand Magellan: Circumnavigating the World* (In the Footsteps of Explorers). Crabtree Publishing Company, 2005.

Gould, Jane H. *Ferdinand Magellan* (Junior Graphic Famous Explorers). PowerKids Press, 2013.

Hoogenboom, Lynn. *Ferdinand Magellan: A Primary Source Biography* (Primary Sources Library of Famous Explorers). PowerKids Press, 2006.

Koestler-Grack, Rachel A. *Ferdinand Magellan* (Great Explorers). Chelsea House Publishers, 2009.

Kramer, Sydelle. *Who Was Ferdinand Magellan?* Grosset and Dunlap, 2004.

October: Magellan continues his voyage with four ships (the *Santiago* sank in a storm).

March 6: Magellan reaches the Pacific island of Guam, where his starving crew get food and water.

April 27: Magellan is killed by native warriors on the island of Mactan while protecting his men.

September 6: The last remaining ship, the *Victoria*, arrives home in Spain with only 18 survivors.

1521

1522

October 21: Magellan enters what is now known as the Strait of Magellan, the narrow passage leading to the Pacific.

March 16: Magellan lands in the Philippines. He converts rulers on some islands to Christianity.

The two surviving ships sail on to the Spice Islands. The *Trinidad* is captured by the Portuguese.

INDEX

31901055876173